Decorating With Silk Flowers

Colorful Arrangements to Accent Your Home

Floral Designer
Allan Howze, AIFD

Contributing Writer
Kathy Lamancusa

Publications International, Ltd.

Allan Howze runs a floral consulting and design firm and is part of the Kennicott Brothers Wholesale Florists Company in Chicago, Illinois. He is a member of the prestigious American Institute of Floral Designers (AIFD) and has studied and taught throughout the U.S., Europe, and the Caribbean.

Kathy Lamancusa is the author of over 20 books and many magazine articles on flower arranging. When not involved in writing and designing, Kathy and her husband present on-stage educational shows for businesses in the floral and craft industries. She is currently vice president of Visual Design Concepts.

Photography: Sacco Productions Limited/Chicago

Photographers: Peter Ross, Peter Walters

Photo Stylist/Production: Melissa J. Sacco, Paula Walters

Models: Karen Blaschek and Cindy Cottrell/Royal Model Management

Photo Site Acknowledgements: The Cotswolds on the Lakes Development, Northbrook, Illinois; Ruth and Robert Sacco; and Eunice Barbee

Copyright © 1993 Publications International, Ltd. All rights reserved. This book may not be reproduced or quoted in whole or in part by mimeograph or any other printed or electronic means, or for presentation on radio, television, videotape, or film without written permission from:

Louis Weber, C.E.O.
Publications International, Ltd.
7373 North Cicero Avenue
Lincolnwood, Illinois 60646

Permission is never granted for commercial purposes.

Manufactured in USA.

8 7 6 5 4 3 2 1

ISBN 0-7853-0102-X

Contents

Introduction	4
Sunny Yellow Centerpiece	12
Profusion of Flowers	14
Asymmetry in Blue	16
Mauve Mantelpiece	18
Americana Basket	20
Spring Wall Hanging	22
Christmas Mantel	24
Southwestern Style	26
One Dozen Roses	28
Holiday Dinner Party	30
European Bouquet	32
Ikebana Arrangement	34
Window Box Floral	36
Victorian Basket	38
Elegant Party Buffet	40
Winter Wonderland	42
Summer Bamboo Basket	44
Table Wreath Centerpiece	46
Flowering Tea Cup	48
Stunning Tropicals	50
Autumn Door Swag	52
Contemporary Tulips	54
Christmas Arch	56
Fruit and Vegetable Basket	58
Romantic Topiary	60
Garden Party	62

Introduction

Flower arrangements have always been welcome additions to any room. But fresh flowers don't last, and ready-made arrangements don't always coordinate with the room or purpose. That's why more people are learning to arrange silk flowers themselves so they can enjoy their accomplishment for more than a few days. And with the variety of new materials available, it is difficult to tell whether your design is made of fresh or silk flowers!

Whether you arrange silk flowers for decorating your home, as a gift, or just for the fun of it, you'll find all the information you need in this book. Begin by learning about the materials and supplies needed. A brief discussion of what you should look for when purchasing silk flowers will help you eliminate mistakes. You'll also learn basic information about designing and forms. Then begin to create captivating silk flower designs by following the step-by-step instructions. Enjoy!

Tips on Purchasing Silk Flowers

When searching for flowers, you may feel overwhelmed with the vast offerings. Differences exist in fabric content, quality, price, and construction. If you understand each of the variables, you can make wise flower purchases.

Fabric Content
Most silk flowers are not silk, but a polyester-type fabric. Many of these flowers are found in the low to midprice range. You will also find a high-end category of flowers that may be pure silk. Usually, these flowers are exquisite and often have been hand painted. Drawbacks to pure silk flowers are longevity and price. They will fade and discolor in direct sunlight, cannot be washed or rinsed, and are usually more expensive.

Quality
Within the two categories of flower fabric content explained above exist many levels of quality differences. Usually the quality differences are evident in the beauty and natural look of the flower. Thinner, poorer quality flowers have droopy petals with ends that are snagged or fraying. Higher quality petals will hold up firmly, appear crisp and sharp, and look more natural.

Price
Silk flower prices can be as low as $.49 per stem with the highest being $12.00 to $15.00 per stem, with many prices in between. The price differences per stem will be based on quality of the fabric, difficulty of achieving the color, amount of color variation per stem, and often the construction of the flower stem itself.

Keep your goal for the silk flower design in mind when deciding on the price range of the flowers. If this will be a design that is seasonal, staying in the mid to low range can be cost effective. However, if you plan this design to be the showpiece in the room, you will probably want to invest in more expensive flowers.

Construction
Silk flowers can be constructed in two ways: handwrapped or polystemmed. Handwrapped stems are the more expensive of the two and are often found on high-end flowers. This method of construction is accomplished by wrapping the pieces of the flower together with floral tape. The entire stem will be wrapped as will each individual flower and leaf. The feel of the stem will be soft and pliable.

Polystemmed flowers are the lower priced category and have plastic stems and plastic knobs to hold the flowers and leaves to the main stem. At times you may find that a flower or leaf falls from the main stem. You should be able to pop it back on, but if it continues to fall off, use craft glue.

Materials and Supplies

It is important to have the proper materials and supplies on hand when you begin arranging silk flowers.

Floral Foams and Mosses

Most floral designs begin with floral foam for inserting the flowers into and moss is used for covering the foam. Three types of foam are available in the market: wet, dry, and plastic. Wet floral foam must be soaked in water before being used and is only appropriate for fresh flower arranging. Dry floral foam has a firmer, sandier consistency and is used exclusively for arranging silk and dried flowers.

Plastic foam is a very firm foam available in green and white. Thinner stemmed dried materials will need to be reinforced with floral tape and stem wire or wired wooden picks before insertion.

Moss is used to cover the foam to hide it from view. A variety of mosses are available. Choose the one that best coordinates with the design you are creating in color and texture.

Flower Arranging Tools

Good quality tools will last for many years. Be prepared by always having the necessary tools close at hand while designing.

Scissors and wire cutters: Wire cutters are used to cut any materials that are made of wire or have a wire core. Scissors should only be used for cutting nonwire objects. They will soon be ruined if you use them to cut wire. Branch cutters are helpful for cutting heavier materials.

Craft knife: A serrated knife is best to cut the blocks of foam.

Ruler or tape measure: These can help when determining the proper length of the stem of a flower or to measure the width and height of your design.

Hot glue gun: Glue guns can be very important to a floral designer. Although white craft glues can also be used, the speed with which hot glue works makes it indispensable. Hot glue sets in 30 to 90 seconds, depending on the amount of glue used. Do be careful, the temperature of the glue can reach 380° and cause painful burns. Caution should be used when creating a design to be used outdoors as hot melt glues are affected by temperature and weather changes.

Floral tools and supplies: 1) dry (above) and plastic (below) floral foam; 2) ⅝″, 1½″, and 2½″ ribbon; 3) floral tape; 4) glue gun; 5) tape measure; 6) wire cutters; 7) floral scissors; 8) branch cutters; 9) spool wire; 10) wooden picks; 11) stapler; 12) tape adhesive; 13) craft knife; 14) craft pins; 15) moss and lichen; 16) chenille stems; 17) stem wire; 18) cloth-covered wire.

Supplies

You will also need a variety of supplies:

U-shaped craft pins: These are known by many different names in various parts of the country—pole pins, greening pins, floral pins. They are used to attach materials to wreaths, help attach ribbons and bows, as well as securing moss to foam.

Straight pins and corsage pins: These are excellent items to have on hand. You'll find a multitude of uses for them.

Stem wire: Wire can be purchased in natural gray as well as painted green. Normally you will be covering the wire with floral tape, so the natural gray is sufficient. It is made in a variety of widths or gauges. The thinner the wire, the larger the gauge of wire: 22-gauge wire is thinner than 16-gauge wire. A 20-gauge wire is perfect to lengthen flower stems as well as help support softer stems.

Cloth-covered wire: This type of wire is wrapped with a threadlike material. It is useful for wiring foam into baskets, securing bows, and attaching florals to wreaths. The cloth-wrapped length of wire is less likely to slip when twisted together. The best gauges to have on hand range from 22 to 28 gauge. It is usually available in green or white.

Chenille stems: You might know them as pipe cleaners. They can be used to attach two pieces of foam, as a hanger, or to secure bows.

Wired wooden picks: A wooden pick has one squared-off end and one pointed end. A wire is attached to the blunt end and is used to wrap around the items that will be secured to the pick.

Tape adhesive: This is a very sticky, puttylike tape for attaching plastic foam to containers. It is also useful when attaching other materials when hot glue is inappropriate.

Floral tape: Floral tape is a waxed crepe paper material in a roll that is used to tape flower stems. The stems of dried materials can be reinforced by floral taping a length of wire to the stem. Flower stems can be lengthened with the same technique.

Selecting and Preparing Containers

Don't limit yourself when choosing a container for your flower arrangement. Anything from an old hat to a crystal bowl could be used. Select a container that has some meaning or sentiment for you: baby shoes, grandad's mug, or an heirloom basket. The floral arrangement and container should complement each other. Neither a casual arrangement in a cut glass vase nor an elegant design done in an antique beer keg are good examples of unity in a design. When selecting the container, try to begin by studying the room in which the design will be placed. Choose a container that matches the nature of the room.

Depending on the type of container selected, you should decide what type of floral design you wish to create. If the container will be the main focal point (such as an antique sewing box), the floral design will be an accent to the container. If the container is plain, the flowers should take the starring role.

The colors in the room will often influence container selection. If purchasing a container to coordinate with the colors in the room, bring along swatches of the colors in the furniture, wall coverings, rug, and drapes to be sure of the color tones you select.

Preparing the container refers to attaching the foam and moss into the container prior to designing. Be sure the foam is slightly smaller than the diameter of the container, about ½" between the foam and basket. The moss will better fit around and can be tucked into the container.

When attaching the foam inside the container, a number of methods can be used. The hot glue gun works well. Be careful, however, of applying it directly to plastic foam as the foam may melt. Tape adhesive also works to attach plastic foam to containers.

If the weave of a basket is too rough and does not create a large enough area to attach the foam, the foam can be wired into the basket. Insert the foam into the basket. Cover it with moss. Cut two pieces of wire twice the height of the floral foam plus ten inches. Bend wires into large *U* shapes and push them through the basket and into the foam about a third of the way from each end. With ends of the wires protruding from the foam, twist one set of wire ends together to hold foam; trim wire ends. Repeat with other wire.

Elements and Principles of Design

Engineering a floral design is based around a specific set of rules and principles. These can be visual as well as technical. The visual aspects help us create a superior design visually; while the technical aspects rule the mechanics of the design to assure that the design is properly prepared. Although we will not be able to see these aspects, they are no less important.

Using Color
Color can be brilliant or dull, vivid or murky. Color can say it all! Color can add a breath of life to a plain design. Emphasis can be added with color, and the designer can draw the eye of the viewer through the design with color.

Since you will be relying on handmade goods and products, color selection can be endless but sometimes inadequate. At times, you will probably feel like no one has just the right color for you.

Keep in mind that you want the colors to blend rather than match. If the dominant color in the room is a medium blue, you will want the flowers you choose to be either deeper or paler in color.

It is best to work with color combinations, as these will help you in the floral selection process. The triad color scheme is popular. These are three colors equally spaced on the color wheel: red, yellow, and blue or green, purple, and orange. You don't have to just use these combinations in their purest form; incorporate tints and shades of these colors: burgundy, golden yellow, and navy.

Often by studying the prints in the furniture, wall coverings, or rugs, you will be able to select a variety of colors to accent the room. These are perfect colors to work with in your silk floral design.

Another popular color scheme is called monochromatic. In this scheme you select one color. Then when designing, add tints and shades of that color. A tint is the color with white added to it. A shade is the color with black added to it. So if you are using red for a monochromatic color scheme, you could also add some pink and some burgundy flowers.

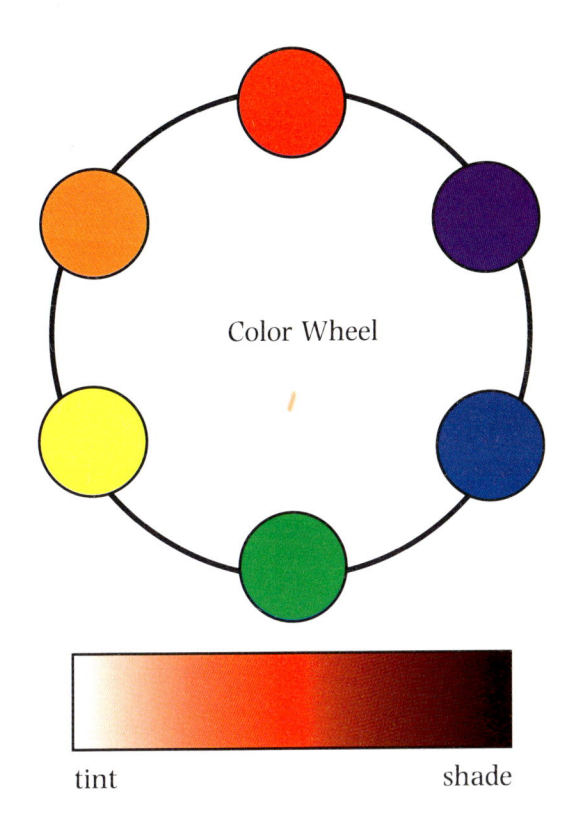

Color Wheel

tint   shade

Complementary colors are those that fall opposite on the color wheel. These color schemes are strong influences on many of our holidays. Red and green are often used for Christmas, while yellow and violet are Easter colors.

Blues, greens, blue-violet, and violet are called cool or receding colors. They produce a calming effect when viewed for extended periods of time. The warm or advancing colors seem to excite us. These colors consist of red, red-violet, oranges, and yellows. Warmer colors are usually used for casual settings and cooler colors are often used for formal locations.

Scale
Every element in a floral design should be in proportion to all of the other elements. A design is in scale when all the elements fit comfortably together—not only in terms of color, but also size.

When beginning an arrangement, you must make many choices, including the size of the container, the number of flowers, amount of filler, and the size of any accent pieces.

Color and texture also play an important role in the selection process. Dark colored materials and items that are used more often take on a greater importance. For example, if you place the larger, darker flowers closer to the center of the design and the smaller, lighter ones on the periphery, your scale is more likely to be correct.

The container should also be appropriate to the scale of the project. The basic rules of design tell us that an arrangement should be at least 1½ to 2 times the height of the container. If the project is in a long, low container, then the same rule applies to the width.

Balance
Balance is the distribution of weight in a design. This must be achieved in two areas: physical and visual. Every design should look and be secure. To assure that the design is stable, proper mechanics are vital. The foam must be properly attached to the container to insure physical stability.

When inserting the flowers into the foam, place flowers so that the entire design does not appear to be falling over. Backward motion is a vital concept. It means that some flowers should be placed behind the central accent location to balance the design from front to back. This will help insure the visual stability.

Unity
Unity is all elements working together. One example is color. When all of the colors used in the design correctly follow a color scheme, they appear unified and therefore create harmony.

Another area to consider is the textures you have chosen to work in the design. Silks, satins, and pearls go together beautifully, as do straw, dried flowers, and rough baskets. However, if you try to put pearls together with straw, harmony and unity are lost. Unity is also created when the elements within are carefully blended and coordinated to work together.

Without consideration for the unity of the finished design, it falls short of its visual goal, which should be to entice the viewer to look longer at the design.

Dominance
Dominance is the difference between the importance of the various materials used. Something should always stand out or dominate each design.

Although the accent of the design is meant to create visual importance, it is not meant to stand out on its own. It should blend with the other elements to create an exciting, unified look to the finished piece. Ninety percent of accent is said to be created by color. Use of the color wheel is an effective aid to come up with color strategies. Often color is the element that attracts the eye.

The use of various textures together in a design will create dominance in the desired areas. For example, if you are creating an Easter design and wish texture to play an important part, use a knobby basket, satin or silk flowers, moss, and fuzzy animals. Accent with several smooth decorated Easter eggs. You'll be amazed at the visual impact you'll create.

A strong vertical, horizontal, or diagonal line can be very dramatic. The effective use of line can accent the elements contained within the design. Space can also be used for accent purposes. Items within a design can be accented merely by leaving adequate space around them to call attention and therefore increase their importance.

Form
Form is an important tool you will be working with as you create your floral designs. To achieve a better understanding of this element, first examine the differences and similarities between shapes and forms.

A shape is known as a geometric form. It is a flat surface having only the thickness of the paper or board from which it is cut or upon which it is drawn. Some shapes are symmetrical and asymmetrical triangles, oblongs or ovals, rounds or circles, and crescents.

A form is a shape that has a third dimension: depth. So that you understand the difference, think of a triangle drawn on a sheet of paper as a shape, and a triangular flower arrangement as a form.

Whenever you design or create, you will work with shapes and forms. One of your first decisions when creating a floral design is what form you wish to create.

Design Forms

The overall form of an arrangement includes its height, width, and depth. It contains the forms and shapes of many individual materials such as flowers and plants, as well as fillers such as ribbons.

Design forms can be broken down into two categories: line designs and curved designs. Each of these categories can be further broken down into two more sections: symmetrical and asymmetrical designs.

Two primary factors influence the type of form that is selected for each individual design: individual preference and the location in which the design will be displayed.

Curved Designs

Curved designs include many styles of circular or rounded forms, such as mounds, ovals, crescents, *S* curves, and mass designs. Line designs are very striking forms that include triangles, verticals, horizontals, *L* shapes, and *T*-shaped designs.

Since a circle is one of the first shapes we learn, it is very pleasing. We seem to enjoy round wreaths on our doors and walls and round floral designs on our tables.

Rounded designs are very versatile. They can be constructed in any size rounded container from the smallest cereal bowl to the largest basket. Rounded designs are perfect to use in the center of the table since all viewers can enjoy the design. Balance is extremely important when creating rounded designs. They should appear uniform in shape with materials equally spaced throughout the design.

The oblong or oval form is useful as an accent within a rectangular shape. An oval flower arrangement balances a rectangular table. When creating a centerpiece, a low, slim container is best. A centerpiece should never exceed 15 inches in height so guests at a table can converse easily.

The mass designs of old were huge displays of multitudes of flowers designed to brighten areas in the homes of the wealthy. Normally they were one sided and designed to fit against a wall or in a corner. The mass designs of today have a look of airy sophistication and are more often seen as full rounded designs that fit into the center of a large table or on a pedestal, placed in an area of prominence. They add an upscale look to our homes and offices.

The crescent and *S* curve are attractive eye-catching designs. They have the greatest potential to move the eye. A crescent or *S*-curved design can accent or call attention to a coordinating piece.

There are many lovely uses for a crescent design. It works well on a table or mantel when the outline of the design repeats the outline of an oval mirror or picture. Round, square, or rectangular containers are good choices for crescent designs as long as they are low.

The *S* curve is a very upright and elegant design and therefore should be used in a place where the design will be a focal point. A tall, cylinder container is the best choice for an *S*-curve design. Sometimes an *S* curve can be created so that the *S* portion is resting

The Victorian Basket is an example of a curved design. It is symmetrically balanced.

The Profusion of Flowers is an upside down *T* shape, also called a triangular form.

on the table. In this way, the two ends would sweep gently around something to which you wish to draw attention.

Line Designs
Line designs consist of any design with a strong line either vertical, horizontal, or diagonal. Usually line designs use few flowers and little foliage and those that are used have exquisite silhouette shapes.

A vertical arrangement is a dynamic style of arrangement and is characterized with tall, vertical flower placements. A tall, narrow container is usually the best used for this type of creation. Keep in mind that vertical designs, as with all line designs, should not be overdeveloped with flowers. Allow the beauty of the flower to be expressed with the use of space around each. When adding flowers, the majority of the placements should not extend over the sides of the container, rather they should appear to be an extension of the container.

Horizontal arrangements are perfect accents when placed under prominent home decorating pieces such as pictures, or when an accent is needed for softness such as on top of a hutch or bureau. The strong horizontal placement of materials makes this design difficult to use in general settings. Long, low containers are normally chosen.

L- and *T*-shaped designs recreate the shape of their name. An *L* design will have strong vertical placements with a shorter horizontal plane extending from the base of the container. A *T* design can either be constructed right side up or inverted. In the traditional design, the shape fits perfectly on top of a wreath with the lower section extending down the center of the wreath and the two side placements being placed on top of the sides of the wreath. An inverted *T* works wonderfully as a table centerpiece.

Symmetrical and Asymmetrical Designs
Symmetrical and asymmetrical designs can be used on a number of the forms explained above. A symmetrical design will be perfectly balanced on both sides of the design. If you were to draw a line down the center of the arrangement, the two sides would be balanced. Asymmetrical designs are balanced in their overall look, but if a line were drawn down the center of the arrangement, the two sides would not be identical. A rounded, mound design is an example of a symmetrical design while an *L* shape will represent the nature of an asymmetrical piece.

Symmetrical designs are usually easier to form, however, asymmetrical creations allow for greater versatility and often a more exciting look. Within a symmetrical design, the placements can be identified as radiating from one central axis point.

Sometimes symmetrical balance is called formal balance, while asymmetrical balance is referred to as informal balance.

Asymmetry in Blue is a *L*-shaped line design. It is a very dynamic arrangement.

The Ikebana Arrangement is a line design. It is a very old arrangement, originally Japanese.

Decorating and Design Tips

• When creating a design, always begin with information you know. What is the color of the room? What is the favorite flower of the person the design is being created for? Is this design for a special holiday or everyday use?

• Remember that deep, dark colors have more visual weight than medium to lighter colors. Visual weight is the size your eye will see that material in relation to other materials of different colors in the design. As an example: a 3 inch wide red rose will appear larger than a 3 inch wide yellow rose.

• Using an unusual type of covering over the floral foam can add interest and excitement to the design. Try shredded marbleized wrapping paper to cover the foam for an elegant den design. Use your imagination.

• Dip the stems of your flowers in glue before inserting them into the floral foam. This will keep them secure in the foam.

• The designs in this book are designed as idea starters. Change the colors or types of materials to create a new feel or look to the design.

• Use colorful accents when creating silk floral designs that stand out. A sudden burst of color is exciting.

• Often a design can be created as an all-year design, but then highlighted for holidays. Insert a heart or shamrock into the design for St. Valentine's or St. Patrick's Day.

• Theming a design can be very important. When creating a design for a new baby girl, use appropriate colors (pink or yellow) coupled with accenting focal pieces such as a pair of baby shoes or a rattle.

• Don't forget that most silk flowers can be washed and blown dry. They will look as good as new. You may also find a silk flower cleaner at your local craft or florist shop.

• A vertical design can be used to accent a candy dish. Simply place floral foam on one side of a flat dish and construct the design so a good amount of the plate is still showing. Fill this area of the plate with candy.

• The smell of potpourri can also add wonderful touches to a design. Create a floral arrangement on one side of a basket and tuck sheets of tissue paper into the empty side of the basket and fill with aromatic potpourri.

• Combining ordinary kitchen utensils, such as wooden spoons, rolling pins, and enamel kettles, can add a delightful look of country to kitchen designs.

• Using two or more arrangements together in a grouping can be a strong visual statement. Form a crescent design on a wreath and hang it above a crescent floral design.

• Victorian designs can be accented with yards of lace and strings of pearls as well as using a variety of green plants.

• Try to make your designs as realistic as possible. Add greenery and other materials so that your designs appear natural.

• Choose a wide variety of shapes and textures for the materials in each design.

• When receiving a special floral design, reserve the container and reuse it to bring back the memory of the gift.

• Keep your eyes open for unusual containers. These could be found at garage sales, flea markets, or even the attic. Often the container can be the focal point of the design.

• When selecting flowers, you should always have one main flower, one secondary flower, and as many filler materials as you wish. The main flower will create the first visual statement of the design while the secondary flower, which should be a different color and texture, will support the main choice.

• Select a design form before you begin. Don't lose track of that form as you work.

• If making a design for your home, keep trying the design in the area where it will be displayed so that you maintain the proper size.

• Above all—Have fun and trust your own imagination!

Sunny Yellow Centerpiece

Often called a "Friendly Bunch," this delightful design is used to create silk arrangements that fit into almost any location, adding color and charm. Since a wide variety of materials can be used, you can change the overall look and feel of this basic round centerpiece merely by changing flowers.

Materials
bowl
dry floral foam
knife
glue gun
green sheet moss
craft pins
wire cutters
5 open yellow roses
4 medium yellow roses
3 stems yellow daisies with 2 flowers each
3 stems miniature white carnations with 2 flowers each
7 stems white baby's breath

1. Cut foam to fit bowl; secure with glue. Using craft pins, cover foam with the green sheet moss.

2. Use wire cutters to cut flowers to desired heights. Establish the height of the arrangement by placing a large open rose (primary flower) in the center of the container. (The size of the flowers will help determine the height of the overall design.) Continue placing four more roses (all the same length) evenly around the base of the container. Fill in the middle with the medium roses.

3. Add the daisies and carnations (secondary flowers) around the arrangement, cutting flower stems so that the flowers create a rounded profile (from all angles). Differently shaped flowers create interest.

4. Cut baby's breath from main stem into pieces. Fill in around primary and secondary flowers with the baby's breath.

Profusion of Flowers

Garden flowers are used to create an elegant, traditional floral design—the basic triangle. When selecting florals be sure to choose a variety of shapes and sizes to create the strongest visual impact. Use the line flowers around the edges and the rounded, mass flowers near the center.

Materials
fireside basket
dry floral foam
knife
green sheet moss
craft pins
22-gauge stem wire
wire cutters
5 stems delphiniums
4 stems carnations with buds
5 stems alstroemeria with 5 flowers
5 stems white asters with 2 flowers
4 stems purple asters with 2 flowers
4 stems eucalyptus foliage

14

1. Cut foam to fit basket and place in basket. Using craft pins, cover foam with sheet moss. Cut two pieces of wire twice the height of the floral foam plus ten inches. Bend wires into a large *U* shape and push them through the basket and into the foam about a third of the way from each end. With both ends of the wire protruding from the foam, twist one set of wire ends together to hold foam. Trim. Repeat with other wire.

2. Establish the height of the arrangement by placing the tallest flower (delphinium) toward the back third of the container in the middle. The height of the tallest element should be at least 1½ to 2 times the height or width of the container—whichever is greater.

3. Create the width with the same flowers (delphinium). Add two more in the middle of the design to carry eye throughout. Add the other flowers to fill in, staggering the heights. Use wire cutters to adjust heights.

4. Add the eucalyptus leaves to complete the triangle shape. All flowers and foliage should appear to radiate from the base of the tallest element.

Asymmetry in Blue

It is important to select flowers and a container that complement each other as well as add accents to your home. The strong use of blue and white in this design is an appealing way to unify the total look. A variety of flowers were chosen to provide contrast and visual excitement to this basic L-shaped arrangement.

Materials

ceramic bowl

dry floral foam

knife

glue gun

green sheet moss

craft pins

wire cutters

3 stems white larkspurs

5 stems blue poppies with 2 flowers each

6 stems blue cornflowers with 3 flowers each

4 stems blue baby's breath with 3 stems each

1. Cut foam to fit bowl, secure with glue. Using craft pins, cover foam with the green sheet moss.

2. Strong vertical and horizontal lines make this design interesting and dramatic. To do that, establish the height of the arrangement by placing the tallest flower (white larkspur) toward the back third of the container. The height of the tallest flower or element should be at least 1½ to 2 times the height or width of the container, whichever is larger. By cutting stems with wire cutters, graduate two more stems of larkspur.

3. Establish the width with the secondary flower (poppy). Make this flower between ½ to ¾ the length of the vertical primary flower. Stagger other flowers inward toward the center of the design. The focal point is at the base of the primary flower.

4. Fill in around primary and secondary flowers with the remaining flowers. All flowers should appear to radiate from the tallest primary flower.

Americana Basket

What could be more appealing than a grouping of apples. This grouping is unique in that it actually creates the form of a basket. Greenery surrounds the handle of the basket adding a needed color and texture change. This basket is the perfect gift for someone with a country-look house!

Materials
wicker basket with handle
green sheet moss
glue gun
22-gauge stem wire
wire cutters
brown floral tape
natural birch branches
branch cutters
about 60 artificial apples
3 pieces of strawberry begonia vine

1. Cut foam to fit bowl, secure with glue. Using craft pins, cover foam with the green sheet moss.

2. Strong vertical and horizontal lines make this design interesting and dramatic. To do that, establish the height of the arrangement by placing the tallest flower (white larkspur) toward the back third of the container. The height of the tallest flower or element should be at least 1 1/2 to 2 times the height or width of the container, whichever is larger. By cutting stems with wire cutters, graduate two more stems of larkspur.

3. Establish the width with the secondary flower (poppy). Make this flower between 1/2 to 3/4 the length of the vertical primary flower. Stagger other flowers inward toward the center of the design. The focal point is at the base of the primary flower.

4. Fill in around primary and secondary flowers with the remaining flowers. All flowers should appear to radiate from the tallest primary flower.

Mauve Mantelpiece

A long, low floral arrangement should be the choice when creating a mantelpiece or hearth design. As the flowers extend outward, they hug the surface, creating visual appeal. Roses were used to contrast with the lilies in shape and color and all were accented by soft, delicate lilac blossoms.

Materials

rectangular container

dry floral foam

knife

glue gun

green sheet moss

craft pins

wire cutters

4 stems delphiniums

5 open roses

3 stems lilies with 2 flowers each

5 stems lilacs with 2 stems each

foliage from lily stems

1. Cut foam to fit container; secure with glue. Using craft pins, cover foam with sheet moss. Establish length of the design by inserting one stem of delphinium on each side of foam.

2. Use wire cutters to cut stems to desired heights. Insert one open rose in middle to establish height. Place some roses around base of container and others coming out from the first rose at an angle. Keep the overall design in mind; you are creating a short triangle with a wide base.

3. Finish design by filling in with the rest of the flowers and foliage. Make sure the same flower types are spaced evenly throughout the design.

Americana Basket

What could be more appealing than a grouping of apples. This grouping is unique in that it actually creates the form of a basket. Greenery surrounds the handle of the basket adding a needed color and texture change. This basket is the perfect gift for someone with a country-look house!

Materials

wicker basket with handle
green sheet moss
glue gun
22-gauge stem wire
wire cutters
brown floral tape
natural birch branches
branch cutters
about 60 artificial apples
3 pieces of strawberry begonia vine

1. Glue sheet moss to outside of the basket. If you wet moss slightly, it will not shed as much as dry moss.

2. Cover a length of wire with brown floral tape. (Stretch tape as you wrap around wire to make tape stick to itself.) Attach natural birch branches to handle of basket using taped wire.

3. Starting with the bottom row, glue artificial apples to moss-covered basket, making sure basket sits evenly. Glue in the next two rows of apples, fitting apples to cover as much area as possible. When gluing apples, be sure to glue sides as well as backs.

4. Cover another length of wire with brown floral tape. Add decorative vines to the handle, securing with taped wire.

21

Spring Wall Hanging

The beauty of nature is depicted in this spectacular spring floral design. Notice the use of twigs as a background and base, contrasted with a plethora of greenery. A few flowers add a visual color statement.

Materials

3 3" clay pots
24-gauge spool wire
wire cutters
dry floral foam
knife
glue gun
green sheet moss
craft pins
3 purple tulips with foliage
3 stems strawberry begonia vines
crocus bulb with 2 flowers
2 stems watermelon begonia vines
2 stems silk wisteria vines
2 stems asparagus ferns
5 to 8 cherry branches (or birch), 36" long
36 strands natural raffia
scissors
20-gauge stem wire
brown floral tape

1. Thread a length of spool wire through drainage hole of each clay pot. Bring wire over lip and twist wire ends together in back of each pot. Make sure wires are long enough to later attach pots to branches.

2. Glue floral foam into clay pots and cover foam with green sheet moss, securing with craft pins. In one pot, glue tulips and strawberry begonia vines. To second pot, glue in crocus and watermelon begonia vines. To last pot, glue in wisteria vines and asparagus ferns. Trail foliage over rims.

3. Clutch branches together ¾ of the way down from the top and tightly bind with spool wire. Divide raffia in half and attach both groups at one end with a knot. Make a simple two loop raffia bow and twist stem wire around center of bow. Attach bow where the branches are bound, bringing wire to back and twisting.

4. Attach the pots to the branches using the long wires. Angle the pots in different directions and fluff the silk flowers as if they have been forced by nature to grow in their angled positions (flowers growing up). Trim wire ends. Cover stem wire with brown floral tape. Twist the wire around a sturdy limb in the back of the design and make a loop for a hanger.

Christmas Mantel

Never think of the elements of design being used only on the floral arrangement itself. Here an asymmetrical appearance is created with the uneven use of the garland on the mantel. The candlesticks then balance the total visual picture and make it complete.

Materials

4 plastic oranges

3 plastic peaches

2 plastic bananas

4 plastic grape clusters

10 pinecones

gold spray paint

4 to 6 pieces Christmas greens (mixed)

glue gun

4 gold mixed holly/berry sprays

10 plastic gold ornaments

3 yards 1½" gold ribbon

25 feet star garland

24

1. Spray fruit and pine cones gold. While paint is drying, place greens on mantel to assemble. You will be making two sections, one for each side of the mantel. If greens are artificial, connect greens by twisting stems together. If greens are real, use spool wire. One side of mantelpiece should hang long, with the other side shorter but thicker.

2. Once you have both sides assembled, take back to your craft table to finish. Mound the gold fruit and glue pieces to the greens. Glue pinecones, berry sprays, and gold ornaments to add different shapes and textures into your design.

3. Entwine ribbon among greens. Unwind gold star garland and loosely attach to the greens.

Southwestern Style

Deep, rich, earth-warmed colors create phenomenal visual impact. Silk lilies form a strong statement when used in the center of the design. The use of cactus and branches along the base create stability and unity. The container has been wrapped with rope giving it a unique feeling and style.

Materials
11½ feet of rope
cylinder container
glue gun
dry floral foam
knife
dry manzanita branches
wire cutters
18-gauge stem wire
10 stems teal reeds
2 burnt orange lilies with 1 bud each
2 dried palmetto leaves
reindeer moss
Spanish moss
3 small barrel cacti

1. Using glue gun, glue natural rope around cylinder container.

2. Cut foam to fit inside container; secure with glue. Cut a 12-inch piece of wire; bend into a *U* shape. Glue ends of wire and use it to secure a manzanita branch into the foam, jutting to the left (craft pins are too short to hold branch).

3. Group reeds together and place in the back middle of the container. This establishes the height of the design. Place lilies in front of reeds.

4. Glue palmetto leaves to the right of the design, at the base of the lilies. Fill in areas where foam shows by gluing reindeer moss and Spanish moss. Glue cacti in front of the lilies.

One Dozen Roses

What could be more pleasing than the gift of a dozen roses. When the roses are made of silk, the gift will be appreciated forever. The design is accented with a wide, simple bow that helps unify the arrangement with its container, as well as adding more color.

Materials

brass container
dry floral foam
knife
glue gun
green sheet moss
craft pins
12 dried-look roses, gold edged
22-gauge spool wire
wire cutters
18″ ribbon (3″ wide)
22-gauge stem wire

1. Cut foam to fit container; secure with glue. Using craft pins, cover foam with the green sheet moss.

2. Clutch ends of roses together; wrap tightly with spool wire.

3. Place roses into middle of foam. Tie a simple bow and use stem wire to attach to rose stems. Trim wire ends.

Holiday Dinner Party

Red and green are the most widely accepted colors for Christmas decorating. In this traditional design, green pine has been mixed with a variety of red materials including poinsettias, berries, and ornaments to make the holiday statement. Personalize your dinner party with the place card holders that echo the centerpiece.

Materials
4" to 6" high brass container
dry floral foam
knife
glue gun
evergreen bough
14 Christmas ornament balls
12 small pinecones
1 spray of plums (or about 7 plums)
4 berry sprays, cut into pieces
3 small poinsettia flowers with leaves

CENTERPIECE

1. Cut floral foam to fit container; glue. (Use a plastic liner if you don't want to glue bowl.) Cut boughs into five to six inch lengths. Form width and length by gluing greens around edge of container.

2. Mound Christmas ornaments, cones, plums, and berry sprays on the greens and floral foam with hot glue.

3. Glue sprigs of greens, poinsettia flowers, and other poinsettia leaves to fill in holes between ornaments and cones.

PLACE CARD HOLDERS

Cut pieces, two to three inch lengths, from bough. Glue sprigs of greens and a few berries to base of ornament, making sure ornament stands upright.

31

European Bouquet

The Europeans portray their love of flowers with the creation of spectacular bouquets using a wide variety of flowers. It is important to have draping materials, such as the ivy shown, as well as an abundance of mass florals to create the bouquet itself.

Materials

vase
glass marbles
wire cutters
10 stems short birch branches
3 stems needlepoint ivy
4 stems pink baby's breath
5 stems white freesia with 3 flowers each
7 open roses
3 stems lilies with buds

1. Partially fill vase with marbles, stones, or glass chips to add weight and stability to the arrangement.

2. Place birch branches to establish height of design. Then insert ivy, baby's breath, and freesia at an angle into the vase to create an anchor for larger flowers. Use wire cutters to stagger heights of flowers.

3. Place roses and lilies into container in order to establish the boundaries for the finished design.

4. Add additional foliage and flowers to fill in the design where needed. Bend ivy so it trails over lip of vase.

Ikebana Arrangement

Minimal use of flowers is the key to creating striking Oriental designs. Each element added to the arrangement should have a strong silhouette to help strengthen the overall design. Flat mushrooms around the low container create a base to balance the finished grouping.

Materials

low ceramic container
dry floral foam
knife
glue gun
green sheet moss
craft pins
wire cutters
3 pieces kiwi vines
2 stems phalaenopsis orchid sprays
2 sansaveria leaves (or other long, thin leaves)
2 pieces shelf mushroom
1 chunk reindeer moss

34

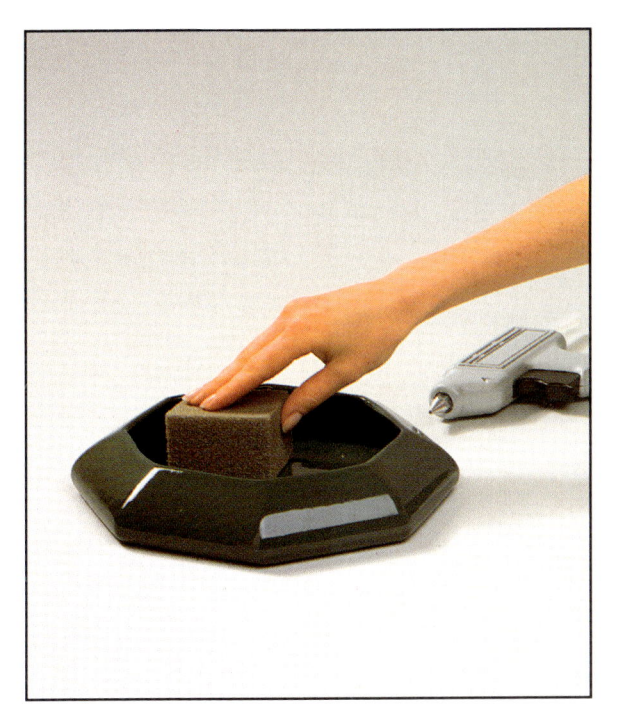

1. Cut a small square of floral foam; place foam to the back and side of the middle of the container. Secure foam in container with glue. Using craft pins, cover foam with sheet moss. Remember that the more foam you have to cover, the busier the design will be. Simplicity is the key to a good, clean design.

2. Glue kiwi vine into the foam to establish height. The top of the tallest kiwi vine should be directly over the point where it is inserted into the foam. Add two more pieces of kiwi vine into the design, both to the left of the first vine with one further front.

3. Add two stems of orchids to the right of the tallest kiwi vine. Glue in leaves a little behind the orchid sprays.

4. Glue mushrooms and reindeer moss to the foam to create visual weight at the base of the design.

Window Box Floral

Designs that remind us of nature are the most appealing in interior design. The use of a variety of greenery around the base helps fill space and create a rich feeling, while stems of florals extend upward to give visual height to this striking design.

Materials

low rectangular wooden planter box
2 blocks dry floral foam
knife
glue gun
green sheet moss
craft pins
wire cutters
2 irises with bud
2 daffodils with bud
1 narcissus with bulb and 2 flowers
1 small cyclamen plant
2 stems yellow teardrops with 2 stems each
1 stem pussy willow (artificial)
1 small woodland fern plant
1 spray needlepoint ivy

1. Cut floral foam to fit into wooden box; secure with glue. Using craft pins, cover foam with sheet moss.

2. Gluing in each flower, place the tallest flower (iris) about ¾ of the way to the right. Place the daffodils to the right of the iris. To the far left, place the narcissus bulb. Behind the narcissus and a bit to the left, add the cyclamen. To the front and right of the narcissus, add the teardrops. Between the iris and the narcissus, place the pussy willow. Keep in mind that you are trying to arrange the plants and flower groupings as if a slice of nature were taken indoors, with like plants grouped together.

3. Glue the fern behind and between the pussy willows and the iris. Glue the ivy in front of the iris. Bend the ivy so that it trails over the edge of the box and make sure that all flowers are growing up.

Victorian Basket

A soft, delicate collar of lace surrounds the basket and becomes an important element for the arrangement. Also, the profusion and different colors, shapes, and sizes of the flowers create a Victorian touch of beauty.

Materials

round basket

3 1/2 feet of lace ribbon (three times circumference of basket)

glue gun

dry floral foam

knife

green sheet moss

craft pins

22-gauge stem wire

wire cutters

3 blue hydrangeas

3 pink roses

7 pansies

3 purple dried-look asters with buds

3 pink dried-look asters with buds

4 stems cream statice with 3 flowers each

2 cream sweet william with buds

2 cream/burgundy sweet william with buds

1. Using the glue gun, glue ribbon around lip of the basket, gathering ribbon as you go. Cut floral foam to fit basket. Using craft pins, cover foam with sheet moss. Cut two pieces of wire twice the height of the floral foam plus ten inches. Bend wire into a large *U* shape and push this up through the basket and into the foam about a third of the way from the end. With both ends of the wire protruding from the foam, twist wire ends together and conceal ends in moss. Repeat with other wire on other end of the foam.

2. Glue all flowers before placing into foam. To establish the perimeter of the design, place the blue hydrangea and the pink roses around the sides. Use wire cutters to cut flowers to desired lengths.

3. Place the pansies and asters to create a rounded shape. Place a few flowers around the perimeter also. If stems of the flowers are too short, add length by floral taping floral picks to the stems.

4. Fill in the design with statice and sweet william.

39

Elegant Party Buffet

Often it is the surprises in the design that create the most memorable touches. Here the use of a champagne bucket as a container adds beauty and excitement. Large, beautiful flowers and leaves help to fill the oversized design of the sky-reaching branches.

Materials

8" extruded foam ball (size depends upon container)
green sheet moss
craft pins
champagne bucket
wire cutters
glue gun
10 birch branches
branch cutters
2 parrot tulips
2 amaryllis with bulb
3 open garden roses
1 stem magnolia with bud
1 stem grape branch
1 stem berry spray (lady apple)
reindeer moss
gray lichen
2 calathea leaves
2 birds
3 birds in nests

40

1. Using craft pins, cover the top of the foam ball with sheet moss. Sit ball securely atop champagne bucket. Glue in all flowers and foliage. Place center branch to establish height. Add rest of branches.

2. Place the parrot tulips toward the back of the design and the amaryllis bulbs toward the front.

3. Place the garden roses throughout, the magnolia flowers to the center front, the grape branch to the left side, and the berry spray to the right side.

4. Glue the moss and lichen to the base to add texture. Glue calathea leaves into the back of the design. Glue birds to the branches; glue a bit of moss over the feet to hide the glue. Glue birds in nests to the base.

41

Winter Wonderland

The clear container has been filled with glass marbles that remind us of ice. The profusion of white materials reinforces the winter theme. Because all the materials are in shades of white and green, selecting materials in different sizes and shapes is important for visual balance.

Materials

glass bowl
dry floral foam
knife
glue gun
glass marbles, chips, or pebbles
3 iridescent white birch branches
wire cutters
4 stems white delphiniums
1 lily
4 stems freesia with 3 flowers each
3 calla lilies
2 stems dendrobium orchid sprays
2 open roses
4 cane springs
4 iridescent ball ornaments

1. Cut a square of floral foam to fit center of bowl; secure with glue. Fill container with glass marbles, chips, or pebbles to hide the foam. Glue in all foliage and flowers. To establish height, place white birch branches in the center back. Stagger heights using wire cutters.

2. Place the delphinium back around birch branches, staggering heights and keeping to the left of the arrangement. Place lily in the center front to create the focal point. To the left and behind the lily, add the freesia. Add calla lilies to the right of the birch branches, staggering heights.

3. Glue orchid sprays in front of the calla lilies, and the roses behind. Turn bowl around; place cane springs behind delphinium, staggering heights.

4. Hot glue ornaments into focal area of the design (around front lily).

43

Summer Bamboo Basket

The trellis was created by using bamboo branches that were tied with raffia and spray painted white. It then was used to accommodate the multitude of blooming roses. The berries and grass complement the beauty of the roses and add movement throughout the design.

Materials
low basket
dry floral foam
knife
green sheet moss
craft pins
18-gauge stem wire
wire cutters
3 pieces bamboo
natural raffia
white spray paint
scissors
glue gun
6 to 8 stems dried-look spray roses
22-gauge stem wire
2 hydrangeas
2 stems berry sprays
dried bear grass
2 stems needlepoint ivy

1. Cut foam to fit basket. Using craft pins, cover foam with green sheet moss. Cut two pieces of 18-gauge wire twice the height of the floral foam plus ten inches. Bend wires into large *U* shapes and push up through the basket and into the foam about a third of the way from each end. With both ends of the wire protruding from the foam, twist one pair of wire ends together to hold foam, then trim wire ends. Repeat with other wire on other end of the foam.

2. Cut bamboo sticks into three uneven pieces. Insert two pieces of bamboo into foam; make a trellis by tying the cross piece with raffia. Pull trellis out of foam and spray paint white. When paint is dry, glue trellis into foam.

3. Wind stems of spray roses onto the left side of the trellis. Use 22-gauge wire to hold roses to trellis, if necessary. Insert one hydrangea flower behind the trellis and one in front, in the center of the design.

4. Add berry sprays in the front center. Stick bear grass into the center and let it spill over the right side of the design. Add ivy to the center back to finish back of the arrangement. Be sure ivy trails over basket.

45

Table Wreath Centerpiece

A wreath becomes the base for a slice of nature. The selection of materials centers around variation in color, texture, and variety to guarantee a look reminiscent of a walk in the woods.

Materials
14" foam wreath
green sheet moss
craft pins
1 mossy/lichen branch
18-gauge stem wire
wire cutters
glue gun
2 stems black-eyed susans with 2 flowers and 1 bud each
2 stems wild garden roses with 1 bud each
3 stems blue allium
2 paphiopedulum orchids or lady slipper orchids
2 Queen Ann's lace with 2 flowers each
2 stems white dogwoods with 2 flowers each
1 spray black/red raspberry
1 stem green berry spray
2 stems blue violets
2 stems ivy
3 clumps reindeer moss
shelf mushroom (cut into pieces)

1. Using craft pins, attach sheet moss to wreath base, covering completely.

2. Attach mossy/lichen branch to wreath by securing with pins made from stem wire and tipped with hot glue before pushing into wreath base (craft pins are too short).

3. For stability, put hot glue on the ends of plants and flower stems before placing into the design. Group like flowers together around base, spacing groupings so that the overall design is balanced.

4. Placing glue on ends of stems, put in the lower plants (raspberry and berry sprays, violets, ivy). Again, keep balance in mind as you place foliage. Add reindeer moss and mushrooms to fill in design and to add texture.

Flowering Tea Cup

A delicate tea cup can become the home of a dainty floral design. Larger, full-sized flowers create the shape of the design with small filler flowers and leaves being used to add depth as well as a contrast in color and texture.

Materials

tea cup and saucer

dry floral foam

knife

glue gun

green sheet moss

craft pins

wire cutters

2 stems ranunculus

1 stem mini artichoke vine

1 stem sweet pea vine with 8 flowers

1. Cut foam to fit cup; secure with glue. Using craft pins, cover foam with the green sheet moss.

2. Glue in ranunculus flowers, creating a small round design. Cut apart artichoke vine and insert pieces (glue before inserting).

3. Cut apart sweet peas and insert to fill in design.

Stunning Tropicals

Large, lush flowers are spectacular when used in entryways, foyers, or even in the bathroom. Because of the size of this type of design, it is important to place it in an area where it has a great deal of space to breathe. Strong lines are created on the vertical as well as horizontal planes, and a focal area flower is stunning.

Materials
purple ceramic cylinder container
dry floral foam
knife
glue gun
green sheet moss
craft pins
wire cutters
2 birds of paradise
2 curly rattan vines
2 purple dendrobium orchid sprays
1 pink protea
2 galax leaves
reindeer moss
gray lichen

50

1. Cut foam to fit container; secure with glue. Using craft pins, cover foam with sheet moss. Glue in all flowers and foliage. Place two birds of paradise vertically to establish height, one taller than the other (use wire cutters to adjust heights).

2. To the left of the birds of paradise, add curly rattan vines. To the right, use two stems of dendrobium orchid sprays to help pull the eye down into the focal area.

3. Complete the design by putting the protea flower in the focal area. Glue in the galax leaves to hide lip of vase. Add moss and lichen to base for texture.

Autumn Door Swag

A study in shiny and dull makes this an interesting hanging for the fall season. The pumpkins contrast well with the shiny look of the brightly colored fall leaves and the greenery attached to the magnolia blossoms. This spectacular design will create a striking statement on your front door.

Materials

3 stems fall leaves
15 stems cattails
3 kiwi vine branches
branch cutters
22-gauge spool wire
wire cutters
1 stem magnolia with bud
2 artificial pumpkins
brown floral tape
22-gauge stem wire

1. Bind fall leaves, cattails, and kiwi vines into separate small bunches, tying each with spool wire about ¾ of the way down.

2. Make a fan shape by clutching the branches in one hand and adding the other bunches on each side. Tie all three together with spool wire. Attach magnolia flowers with wire on the opposite side of the leaves. (Cattails become the center.)

3. Hot glue artificial pumpkins below leaves and flowers, creating the focal point of the design.

4. For hanger, cover stem wire with brown floral tape. Twist the wire around a sturdy branch in the back (make sure wire ends are behind branch). Twist again to make a loop.

53

Contemporary Tulips

This long, slim design is an elegant lesson in movement and style. Thin slivers of greenery help widen the visual appeal at the base of the design, while the grapes form an anchor for the majestic tulips. The branches create spectacular height.

Materials
brass or ceramic bubble container
dry floral foam
knife
glue gun
green sheet moss
craft pins
wire cutters
2 dried fantail willow branches
2 tulips with foliage
1 cluster of isolepsis grass
1 cluster of grapes
1 stem of rose spray
4" wooden floral picks
floral tape

54

1. Cut foam to fit container; glue. Using craft pins, cover foam with sheet moss. Glue in all flowers and foliage. Establish height with dried fantail willow. The top of the fantail willow should be directly over the point where it is inserted into the foam. Add shorter second branch to the right. Use wire cutters to adjust heights.

2. Add two tulips (cut leaves off) at different heights to the left of the willow. Cluster isolepsis grass and wrap wire around grass and pick. Tape over with floral tape. Insert isolepsis grass to the left of the tulips and glue tulip leaves to moss. Treat foliage as if they were flowers; they become actual elements of the design.

3. Glue a grape cluster to the front center. Remove rose heads from spray and glue a cluster of flower heads at the back.

Christmas Arch

Floral arches can be used in a multitude of ways—they welcome guests in our homes with a pleasant statement of elegance and beauty or they can add a Christmas touch to a foyer. Pine was used as a background for this Christmas arch, while a glittering tapestry bow, branches of red berries, and stems of cinnamon sticks add the finishing touches.

Materials

30″ Christmas greens wreath
36″ ribbon (3″ wide)
22-gauge stem wire
glue gun
8 berry sprays
brown floral tape
14 to 16 cinnamon sticks
18 small to medium pinecones
wire cutters

1. Bend the wreath in half.

2. Combine the two pieces to make a half circle or arch by twisting pieces of the wired greens together. Make a two loop bow by measuring the desired tail length from the end of the ribbon and making a loop on each side of your thumb. Twist stem wire around center of bow to hold shape, bring wire to back.

3. Fluff the branches of the arch. Use wires to attach bow to the center of the arch. If berry sprays are not long enough, wrap floral tape around the end of the spray and attach a length of stem wire. Glue cinnamon sticks, berry sprays, and cones jutting out from each side of the bow.

4. Taper the ends of the arch by snipping off sprigs with wire cutters. To attach hanger, cover stem wire with brown floral tape. Twist the wire around the middle of the heavy wire of the wreath in the back and twist to make a loop.

Fruit and Vegetable Basket

The casual look of a basket of fruit and vegetables is legendary in home decoration. The materials available in the marketplace today allow for tremendous creativity in the creation of the basket. The materials are so lifelike, someone may even be tempted to take a bite! Remember to use a wide variety of colors and shapes.

Materials
low oval wicker basket (11" × 5")
dry floral foam
knife
green sheet moss
craft pins
22-gauge stem wire
wire cutters
fruit and vegetable pieces of various sizes (12 to 15 pieces)
awl
wooden picks
glue gun
3 berry sprays
4 stems needlepoint ivy

1. Cut floral foam to fit basket. Using craft pins, cover foam with sheet moss. Cut two pieces of wire twice the height of the floral foam plus ten inches. Bend wires into large *U* shapes and push up through the basket and into the foam about a third of the way from each end. With both ends of the wire protruding from the foam, twist one pair of wire ends together to hold foam, then trim wire ends. Repeat with other wire. Carefully make small holes in all fruit and vegetable pieces with an awl. Remove wire from wooden picks and insert into fruit and vegetable pieces (glue if necessary).

2. Glue fruit and vegetables into basket, arranging them so that the weight of the design is balanced. Some fruit should hang over the lip of the basket.

3. Cut berry sprays into sprigs and ivy into smaller pieces. Glue in berry sprigs and ivy. Some ivy should trail down edges of basket.

59

Romantic Topiary

Topiaries were brought to us from Victorian times. Their traditional look makes an exciting statement no matter what materials are used to create them. Here long stems of silk blossoms are bound together forming a treelike design. Ivy secured around the base stabilizes and unifies.

Materials

5" clay pot
gold spray paint
dry floral foam
knife
glue gun
green sheet moss
craft pins
5 stems delphiniums
wire cutters
22-gauge spool wire
18" ribbon for bow (3" wide)
22-gauge stem wire
scissors
2 stems ivy, cut into pieces

1. Tint the clay pot by lightly spraying gold paint from a distance.

2. Cut floral foam to fit pot; secure with glue. Using craft pins, cover top of foam with green sheet moss. Tie five stems of delphiniums together with spool wire below foliage. Insert flowers into the middle of the pot. Trim some of the lower foliage off.

3. Make a simple bow by creating two loops with ends hanging; use stem wire to fasten bow in center. With wire, tie all stems together beneath foliage. Trim wire ends.

4. Glue ivy into pot and bend ivy so it trails over rim of the pot.

61

Garden Party

Clay pots can help us recall gardens, nature, and the beauty and fulfillment of planting and growing. Votive candles add soft light and the leaf place mats complete the fun and fantasy.

Materials

8 3" clay pots
dry floral foam
knife
glue gun
green sheet moss
craft pins
wire cutters
2 stems irises
reindeer moss
trailing lichen
1 stem crocus with bulb and 2 flowers
1 stem kale
1 stem yellow forsythia branch
2 stems yellow roses with 2 flowers each
2 stems lilacs
shelf mushroom
1 bird
1 bird in nest
1 yard green material
1 large ivy plant (with large leaves)
1 spray needlepoint ivy
3 votive candles

1. Cut foam to fit five clay pots; secure with glue. Using craft pins, cover the foam with the green sheet moss.

2. Glue the irises, reindeer moss, and trailing lichen into one pot; the crocus into another; kale into another; forsythia branch into another; and the roses and lilacs into the last.

3. Spread green sheet moss onto center of table and scatter pots on top of the moss. Tip some of the pots on the side to add interest. Bend flowers or plants in the tipped pots so they look as if they would be growing (pointed up).

4. Add pieces of mushroom, bird, and nest into the design.

PLACE MATS

1. Cut fabric into 12" × 16" pieces.

2. Cut leaves off an ivy plant or any other type of plant with large leaves. Start at one end of the fabric and staple or hot glue leaves in a row. Each row of leaves will overlap and hide the glue or staples.

CANDLE HOLDERS

1. Secure a small amount of dry foam into bottom of three small clay pots; cover foam with sheet moss using craft pins. Place a votive candle into each pot.

2. Glue in small pieces of ivy so they trail over the edge of the pots. Add votive candles to centerpiece.